I0012827

The AI Survival Guide for Small Businesses

Introduction

In today's rapidly evolving business landscape, companies of all sizes face unprecedented challenges. The digital revolution has leveled the playing field in many ways, but it has also introduced new complexities and competitive pressures. Among the most transformative technologies of our time, Artificial Intelligence (AI) stands out as a potential game-changer for businesses looking to boost efficiency, save time, and grow revenue.

The AI revolution is not just for tech giants or multinational corporations. Small and medium-sized businesses can now leverage AI to punch above their weight and carve out new niches in their markets. This book will show you how to seize that opportunity, regardless of your technical expertise or the size of your IT budget.

These pages are designed to be your comprehensive guide to understanding and implementing AI in your company, whether you own a small local shop or a growing mid-sized enterprise. As a business owner, manager, or entrepreneur, you'll gain the knowledge and strategies needed to harness the power of AI and stay competitive in an increasingly AI-driven world.

Throughout this book, we'll explore how AI can revolutionize various aspects of your operations, from customer service and marketing to financial management and decision-making. Along the way, we'll also demystify AI technologies, discuss practical applications, and provide real-world case studies of businesses that have successfully leveraged AI to transform their operations. Each chapter is designed to provide actionable insights and strategies that you can begin implementing right away.

You don't need to be a tech expert to benefit from the insights in this book, as we've written it with the non-technical business leader in mind. We will explain AI's complexities in clear, accessible language. At the same time, we dive deep enough to provide real value to those who may already have some familiarity with AI.

As we embark on this journey together, remember that the goal is not to implement AI for its own sake but to leverage it as a powerful tool that can help you achieve your business objectives, enhance your value proposition, and better serve your customers. The AI revolution is here, and with the knowledge and strategies provided in this book, your business will be at the forefront of this exciting transformation.

Welcome to the AI revolution for businesses of all sizes!

Chapter 1

Understanding AI for Your Business

Artificial Intelligence (AI) has become a buzzword in the business world, but what does it really mean for your company?

At its core, AI refers to computer systems designed to perform tasks that typically require human intelligence, such as visual perception, speech recognition, decision-making, and language translation. As such, AI is not a single technology but rather a broad field encompassing various approaches and techniques.

The Fundamentals of AI

To truly understand how AI can benefit your business, you must understand its fundamental components, which are described in detail below.

- **Machine Learning (ML)** is a subset of AI where systems use experience to improve their performance on a specific task. Unlike traditional software that follows pre-programmed rules, ML algorithms can analyze data, identify patterns, and make predictions without being explicitly programmed to do so. For example, you could use an ML system to analyze your sales data to predict future demand, and it will become more accurate over time as it processes more information.

- **Deep Learning** is a more advanced form of machine learning that uses neural networks with multiple layers (hence "deep") to analyze multiple data factors simultaneously. Deep learning is particularly powerful for tasks like image and speech recognition. In a business

You don't need to be a tech expert to benefit from the insights in this book, as we've written it with the non-technical business leader in mind. We will explain AI's complexities in clear, accessible language. At the same time, we dive deep enough to provide real value to those who may already have some familiarity with AI.

As we embark on this journey together, remember that the goal is not to implement AI for its own sake but to leverage it as a powerful tool that can help you achieve your business objectives, enhance your value proposition, and better serve your customers. The AI revolution is here, and with the knowledge and strategies provided in this book, your business will be at the forefront of this exciting transformation.

Welcome to the AI revolution for businesses of all sizes!

Chapter 1

Understanding AI for Your Business

Artificial Intelligence (AI) has become a buzzword in the business world, but what does it really mean for your company?

At its core, AI refers to computer systems designed to perform tasks that typically require human intelligence, such as visual perception, speech recognition, decision-making, and language translation. As such, AI is not a single technology but rather a broad field encompassing various approaches and techniques.

The Fundamentals of AI

To truly understand how AI can benefit your business, you must understand its fundamental components, which are described in detail below.

- **Machine Learning (ML)** is a subset of AI where systems use experience to improve their performance on a specific task. Unlike traditional software that follows pre-programmed rules, ML algorithms can analyze data, identify patterns, and make predictions without being explicitly programmed to do so. For example, you could use an ML system to analyze your sales data to predict future demand, and it will become more accurate over time as it processes more information.

- **Deep Learning** is a more advanced form of machine learning that uses neural networks with multiple layers (hence "deep") to analyze multiple data factors simultaneously. Deep learning is particularly powerful for tasks like image and speech recognition. In a business context, you could use deep learning systems for tasks such as analyzing customer sentiment from social media posts or identifying defects in manufacturing processes by using image analysis.

- **Natural Language Processing (NLP)** allows machines to understand, interpret, and generate human language. This technology powers chatbots, voice assistants, and automated translation services. For your business, NLP could enable more efficient customer service, automate email sorting and response, or even help analyze customer feedback at scale.

- **Computer Vision** gives machines the ability to interpret and understand visual information. It has a wide range of business applications, such as quality control in manufacturing, automated checkout systems, and the analysis of foot traffic patterns in retail stores.

AI in Action: Practical Applications for Your Business

Now that we've covered the basics, we will explore how these AI technologies can be applied to solve real business problems:

Its first application is in **predictive analytics**. By analyzing historical data, AI can forecast trends, customer behavior, and business outcomes, which can be invaluable for inventory management, sales forecasting, and customer retention strategies. For instance, a clothing retailer could use predictive analytics to optimize their stock levels based on factors such as seasonal trends, weather forecasts, and social media buzz.

The next important application is **conversational AI**. Chatbots and virtual assistants can handle customer inquiries, schedule appointments, and even assist with sales by providing 24/7 customer service without the need for a large staff. This technology can be particularly beneficial for small businesses looking to provide round-the-clock support without the overhead of a large customer service team.

AI is particularly good at **process automation**. It can automate repetitive tasks across various business functions, from data entry to complex financial analyses, freeing up human resources for more strategic work. For example, an accounting firm could use AI to automate expense categorization and the generation of financial reports, allowing its staff to focus on higher-value activities like financial strategy and advising clients.

Finally, AI can be used as a **recommendation system**. These AI systems can suggest products or services to customers based on their preferences and behavior, potentially increasing sales and customer satisfaction. E-commerce businesses, in particular, can benefit from this aspect of AI technology to provide personalized shopping experiences and increase cross-selling opportunities.

The Current State of AI Adoption

As of 2024, AI adoption among businesses is growing rapidly, but there is still significant room for expansion. According to recent surveys:

- Approximately 33% of companies invested in AI in 2023.[1]

---

[1] "AI and SMBs: An Analysis of Their Adoption and Impact," Microsoft News Centre Canada, April 19, 2024, accessed July 10, 2024, https://news.microsoft.com/en-ca/2024/04/19/ai-and-smbs-an-analysis-of-their-adoption-and-impact/#:~:text=For%20the%20surveyed%20compan ies%2C%20investment,start%20investing%20in%20AI%20in.

- Approximately 71% of businesses plan to continue or start investing in AI in the near future.[2]
- The primary focus of AI investment for businesses is improving customer service satisfaction (50%) and efficiency (51%).[3]

The statistics show that many small and medium businesses are increasingly recognizing the potential of AI to level the playing field with larger competitors. However, adoption rates vary by industry and region, with tech-savvy sectors and developed economies generally leading the way. The challenge for you, as a business owner, is to bridge the gap and fully harness the incredible advantages that AI offers, ensuring your business remains competitive and innovative.

Overcoming Common Misconceptions

Despite its potential, many business owners have reservations about adopting AI. These concerns combine to create a cautious approach towards AI adoption, even as its advantages become increasingly evident.

Here are a few of the most common misconceptions:

- **"AI is too expensive for smaller companies":** While some AI solutions can be costly, there are many affordable options designed specifically for small and medium-sized businesses. Cloud-based AI services, in particular, have

---

[2] Todd Lohr et al., "Generative AI: From Buzz to Business Value," KPMG, May 2023, accessed July 10, 2024, https://kpmg.com/kpmg-us/content/dam/kpmg/pdf/2023/generative-ai-survey.pdf.

[3] "Marketers Say AI's ROI Isn't Just About Financial Gain," Marketing Charts, April 12, 2024, accessed July 10, 2024, https://www.marketingcharts.com/customer-centric/analytics-automated-and-martech-232600.

made advanced AI capabilities accessible to businesses of all sizes.

- **"AI will replace human workers"**: In reality, AI often augments human capabilities rather than replacing them entirely. It typically takes over repetitive tasks, allowing employees to focus on more creative and strategic work. The key is to view AI as a tool to enhance your workforce, not replace it.

- **"AI is too complex for non-tech businesses"**: Many AI tools are designed to be user-friendly and don't require extensive technical knowledge to implement and use effectively. The focus should be on understanding how AI can solve your specific business problems, not on the technical details of how it works.

- **"Our business is too small to benefit from AI"**: Even the smallest businesses can benefit from AI in areas like customer service, marketing, and operations. The key is to start small and pinpoint the specific areas where AI can provide immediate value.

- **"AI requires too much data to be effective"**: While more data can improve AI performance, many AI tools can work effectively with the amount of data typically available to small and medium-sized businesses. The quality of data is often more important than the quantity.

As we move forward in this book, we'll explore how businesses of all sizes can overcome these misconceptions and leverage AI to drive growth, improve efficiency, and stay competitive in an increasingly digital world. The key is to approach AI adoption strategically, focus on the specific business problems that AI can help solve, and consider the long-term benefits.

Most importantly, you must be ready to adopt AI technologies. Your readiness will lay the groundwork for a successful AI implementation strategy, a crucial step that we describe in detail in the next chapter.

Chapter 2

Assessing Your Business's AI Readiness

Before implementing AI, you must assess your company's readiness for this transformative technology. This chapter will guide you through evaluating your current business processes by helping you identify areas where AI can make the most impact, assess your team's AI skills, and create an AI adoption roadmap.

Evaluating Your Current Business Processes

The first step in assessing AI readiness is to examine your existing business processes thoroughly. This evaluation will help you identify inefficiencies and areas where AI could potentially streamline operations.

Begin by creating a detailed map of your business processes across all departments, including customer acquisition and retention processes, product development and delivery workflows, financial management procedures, and internal communication systems.

Consider using process mapping tools or even simple flowcharts to visualize these processes.

For example, in your customer service department, you might map out the journey from initial customer contact to issue resolution. Doing so could reveal bottlenecks where AI could be applied, such as using natural language processing to categorize and route customer inquiries automatically.

Next, evaluate the quality and quantity of data your business currently collects and manages. AI thrives on data, so understanding your data landscape is crucial. Consider what types of data you collect, how it's stored and managed, and its overall quality and consistency.

Ask yourself the following questions:

- What customer data do we collect, and how is it used?
- How do we track and analyze sales data?
- What operational data do we gather from our day-to-day processes?
- How consistent and accurate is our data across different systems?

For instance, an e-commerce business might find it has rich data on customer purchasing history and browsing behavior but needs more information on customer service interactions. Understanding this lack should convince the business owner to consider using AI for personalized product recommendations while also highlighting the need to improve data collection in customer service before implementing any AI systems.

Finally, assess your current technology infrastructure. Ask yourself these questions.

- What software and hardware are you currently using?
- How well do your systems integrate?
- Are there any significant technology gaps or outdated systems that might hinder AI adoption?

Then consider creating a technology inventory, noting the following:

- Current software systems (CRM, ERP, etc.) and their capabilities.

- Hardware infrastructure (servers, networks, etc.).
- Data storage and management systems.
- Current level of cloud adoption.
- Integration between various systems.

Your initial assessment might reveal, for example, that your current CRM system doesn't easily integrate with other tools, posing a challenge for implementing AI across customer-facing processes. Early identification of these issues allows you to address them as part of your AI adoption strategy.

Identifying Areas Where AI Can Make the Most Impact

Once you have a clear picture of your current processes, the next step is to identify areas where AI can provide the most significant benefits. Look for processes that involve repetitive, rule-based tasks, as these are often prime candidates for AI automation.

For example, in a financial services firm, the process of reviewing loan applications often involves repetitive checks of credit scores, income verification, and risk assessment. These tasks are excellent candidates for AI automation, which could speed up the process and improve consistency.

Also, consider areas where large amounts of data are processed manually. AI excels at quickly analyzing vast datasets, potentially uncovering insights that humans might miss. A retail business, for instance, might benefit from AI-powered inventory management that can analyze sales data, market trends, and even weather forecasts to optimize stock levels.

Customer interactions are another area where AI can have a significant impact. Consider touchpoints where AI could help you enhance the customer experience, such as through chatbots or personalized recommendations. For example, an online retailer might implement an AI chatbot to handle common customer queries, freeing up human agents to deal with more complex issues.

Look for areas where decisions are made based on data analysis, as AI can often improve the speed and accuracy of these decisions. Thus, a manufacturing company might use AI to analyze production data and predict when machinery is likely to need maintenance, allowing for proactive repairs and reducing downtime.

Finally, identify areas where prediction could improve operations, such as inventory management or sales forecasting. AI's predictive capabilities can provide valuable insights in these areas, helping businesses to be more proactive and efficient.

Assessing Your Team's AI Skills and Knowledge

Before implementing AI technologies, you must understand your team's current capabilities. Conducting a survey can help you discover the team's current understanding of AI concepts and experience with AI tools.

Use the survey to assess your employees':

- General understanding of AI and its potential applications in business.
- Familiarity with data analysis and statistical concepts.
- Experience with any AI or machine learning tools.
- Programming skills, particularly in languages commonly used in AI (like Python or R).
- Understanding of data privacy and ethical considerations in AI.

You might find, for example, that while your IT team has a solid grasp of AI concepts, your marketing team needs to become more familiar with how AI could benefit their work. This insight can help you tailor your AI training and implementation strategies to the skills and experience level of each team.

Additionally, look for team members who show enthusiasm for AI and could lead implementation efforts. These "AI champions" can play a crucial role in driving adoption across the organization.

Creating an AI Adoption Roadmap

With a clear understanding of your current processes, potential AI applications, and team capabilities, you can now create a roadmap for AI adoption.

Based on potential impact and ease of implementation, prioritize your AI initiatives. For each AI project, define specific, measurable objectives. What do you hope to achieve with AI implementation? Be as specific as possible. For example, "Implement an AI chatbot to reduce customer service response times by 50% within six months."

Use the following process to create the most efficient AI implementation strategy for your business.

1. **Determine** what resources (budget, personnel, time) you can allocate to AI initiatives and create a realistic timeline for implementation, considering factors like training needs and potential disruptions to current processes.

2. **Identify** potential risks and challenges in AI adoption and develop mitigation strategies. These might include data privacy concerns, integration issues with existing systems, or employee resistance to new technologies.

3. **Define** key performance indicators (KPIs) to measure the success of your AI initiatives. These could include metrics

like cost savings, productivity improvements, or customer satisfaction scores.

4. **Start with** a small-scale pilot project, which will allow you to learn and adjust before broader implementation. This approach can help you demonstrate AI's value to stakeholders and build momentum for broader adoption.

Case Study: Woodside Energy

Before finishing this chapter, let's look at how a real business approached the AI implementation process. Woodside Energy, an Australian-based oil, gas, and new energy company began the process by determining its goals and assessing its AI readiness. They identified operating expenses as an area where AI could have a significant impact.

They set a goal of reducing their operating expenses by 30% by implementing technology sustainably and strategically. They also decided to incorporate the following concepts into their AI rollout:

- Automated contract management
- Material optimization
- Inventory management
- Predictive maintenance

Woodside Energy's initiatives are estimated to reduce operating expenses by approximately AUD 110 million per year. The company also continues to scale the project and has identified over 30 initiatives to expand.

By thoroughly assessing your business's AI readiness, you can ensure that your AI adoption journey is strategic, focused, and aligned with your business goals. This preparation will significantly increase your chances of successful AI implementation and maximize your business's benefits.

In Chapter 3, we will explore how to start implementing AI in your business, beginning with one of the most immediately impactful applications: automating routine tasks.

Chapter 3

Automating Routine Tasks with AI

One of the most immediate and impactful ways businesses can leverage AI is through the automation of routine tasks. This chapter explores how AI-driven automation can significantly improve efficiency, reduce errors, and free up valuable human resources for more strategic work.

Understanding AI-Powered Task Automation

AI-powered task automation goes beyond traditional rule-based automation. It can adapt to changing conditions, learn from data, and handle more complex tasks that previously required human intervention.

The benefits of AI automation are substantial and include the following:

- **Increased Efficiency:** AI can perform tasks faster and more consistently than humans. It is often available 24/7.
- **Reduced Errors:** AI minimizes human errors in repetitive tasks.
- **Cost Savings:** Automating routine tasks can lead to significant labor cost reductions.
- **Improved Employee Satisfaction:** By taking over mundane tasks, AI allows employees to focus on more engaging and valuable work.
- **Scalability:** AI systems can easily scale to handle increased workloads without proportional increases in cost.

Now, let's examine some specific areas where AI automation can significantly impact your business.

Administrative Tasks

Many administrative tasks are ripe for AI automation. For example, AI can revolutionize email management by automatically categorizing, prioritizing, and even drafting responses to routine inquiries. In financial administration, AI can automate invoice processing by extracting relevant data, verifying it against purchase orders, and facilitating payment approval workflows. Finally, AI-driven chatbots and virtual assistants can handle routine customer service queries, providing instant responses to frequently asked questions and escalating more complex issues to human agents when necessary.

To implement a similar system in your business, start by analyzing your administrative needs. Consider areas such as data entry, document management, communication handling (like emails and customer queries), scheduling, and financial administration. Then, engage with key stakeholders, evaluate available AI technologies and solutions that align with your requirements, and develop a comprehensive implementation plan.

Financial Processes

AI can dramatically streamline financial processes, from bookkeeping to fraud detection. For smaller businesses, AI-powered accounting software can automate tasks like data entry, reconciliation, and even basic financial reporting.

When implementing such a system, start with a clear audit of your current financial processes. Identify the most time-consuming tasks and those most prone to human error. These are likely the best candidates for AI automation.

Customer Service

AI-powered chatbots and virtual assistants can handle a significant portion of customer inquiries, providing 24/7 support requiring a large staff. These intelligent systems use NLP to understand and respond to customer queries promptly and accurately. By leveraging AI, small and medium businesses can offer immediate responses to frequently asked questions, assist with order tracking, process returns or exchanges, and provide personalized recommendations based on customer preferences and past interactions.

When implementing a chatbot, start by analyzing your most common customer inquiries. Use this data to train your AI system. Remember, the goal is not to replace human customer service entirely but to augment it, allowing your team to provide better service on complicated issues.

Inventory Management

AI can revolutionize inventory management, especially for businesses dealing with a large number of SKUs or perishable goods. By utilizing machine learning algorithms, AI can analyze historical sales data, seasonal trends, and external factors such as weather patterns or economic conditions to forecast demand with greater accuracy. This predictive capability allows small and medium businesses to optimize their inventory levels and automate replenishment processes. Additionally, AI-powered systems can monitor inventory in real-time, alerting warehouse managers to potential issues such as overstocking, slow-moving items, or anomalies that may require immediate attention.

To implement an AI inventory management system, start by ensuring you have good-quality historical data on your inventory levels and sales. The more data you have, the more accurate your AI predictions will be. Then, select the AI algorithms that are suitable for your specific business needs. Integrate these algorithms with your existing inventory management software while closely collaborating with your IT and operations teams to ensure smooth implementation and integration of the AI system into daily workflows.

Implementation Strategies and Best Practices

When implementing AI for task automation, you should use the following strategies:

1. **Start Small:** Begin with a pilot project in one area of your business, which will allow you to learn and adjust before implementing it widely.
2. **Choose the Right Tasks:** Focus on high-volume, rule-based tasks that don't require complex decision-making or emotional intelligence.
3. **Ensure Data Quality:** AI systems rely on good data. Ensure your data is clean, organized, and accessible.
4. **Involve Your Team:** Engage employees in the automation process. They often have valuable insights into which tasks are most suitable for automation.
5. **Provide Training:** Offer training to help employees work alongside AI systems effectively.
6. **Monitor and Optimize:** Continuously track the performance of your AI automation and make adjustments as needed.
7. **Consider Integration:** Ensure new AI tools can integrate with your existing systems for seamless operations.
8. **Plan for Exceptions:** Develop processes for handling exceptions or situations where the AI system may not be able to complete a task.
9. **Prioritize Security:** Implement robust security measures to protect sensitive data processed by AI systems.
10. **Stay Compliant:** Ensure your AI automation adheres to relevant regulations and industry standards.

Overcoming Common Challenges

As you implement AI automation, you may encounter some challenges. Below, we highlight the most common and explain how to mitigate them.

- **Resistance to Change:** Address employee concerns about job security and emphasize how AI will enhance their work rather than replace them.
- **Technical Hurdles:** Be prepared for potential technical issues during implementation. Have IT support ready and consider working with AI consultants.
- **Data Privacy Concerns:** Implement strong data protection measures and be transparent about how data is used in AI systems.
- **Overreliance on AI:** Encourage critical thinking and human oversight to avoid mindlessly trusting AI outputs.
- **Scalability Issues:** Ensure your chosen AI solutions can scale as your business grows.

The Future of AI Task Automation

As AI technology continues to advance, we can expect to see:

- **More Accessible AI Tools:** Increasing availability of user-friendly, affordable AI tools designed specifically for small and medium-sized businesses.
- **Enhanced Natural Language Processing:** Improving the ability of AI to understand and generate human-like text, enabling more complex task automation.
- **Greater Integration:** Creating seamless integration of AI automation across various business functions and systems.
- **Predictive Automation:** Anticipating needs and proactively automating tasks.

- **Collaborative AI:** Generating advanced AI assistants that can work alongside humans in more complex, creative tasks.

By strategically implementing AI-driven task automation, small and medium businesses can significantly enhance their operational efficiency, reduce costs, and free up human resources for more valuable, strategic work. As you move forward with automation, remember to approach it as a gradual process, continually learning and adapting your approach to best suit your business's needs.

In the next chapter, we'll explore how AI can be leveraged to enhance the customer experience, a critical factor for your business's success in today's competitive landscape.

Chapter 4

Enhancing Customer Experience Through AI

In today's competitive business landscape, providing an exceptional customer experience is critical for creating your brand. This chapter explores how AI can revolutionize customer interactions, personalize experiences, and ultimately drive customer satisfaction and loyalty.

The Power of AI in Customer Experience

We will begin by examining how AI can AI transform every aspect of the customer journey, from initial engagement to post-purchase support.

1. Personalization at Scale

AI enables businesses to provide highly personalized experiences to each customer, something that would be impossible to do manually at scale.

To implement a similar system in your business:
1. Start by consolidating your customer data from various sources (e.g., website interactions, purchase history, customer service interactions).
2. Choose an AI-powered personalization platform that integrates with your existing e-commerce and email marketing systems.
3. Begin with simple personalization (such as product recommendations) and gradually increase the complexity as you gather more data and refine your approach.

Remember, the key to effective personalization is respecting customer privacy. Be transparent about data usage and always provide opt-out options.

2. 24/7 Customer Support with AI Chatbots

AI-powered chatbots can handle a significant portion of customer inquiries, providing round-the-clock support without the need for a large staff.

To implement an effective AI chatbot in your business:

1. Analyze your most common customer inquiries and use this data to train your chatbot.
2. Start with a limited scope (for example, handling FAQs) and expand capabilities over time.
3. Ensure the technology allows for a smooth handoff to human agents for complex issues.
4. Continuously monitor chatbot performance and user feedback to improve its effectiveness.

3. Predictive Customer Service

AI can anticipate customer needs and potential issues before they arise, allowing businesses to provide proactive support.

To implement predictive customer service in your business:

1. Identify data sources that can provide early indicators of potential issues (e.g., product usage data, customer behavior patterns).
2. Implement an AI system that can analyze this data and generate actionable insights.
3. Develop processes for your team to act on these insights proactively.

4. Voice AI and Natural Language Processing

Advanced NLP is making customer interactions more natural and efficient.

To implement voice AI in your business:
1. Start by identifying the most common reasons customers call your business.
2. Choose an NLP platform that supports the languages your customers speak.
3. Begin with simple voice interactions and gradually increase complexity.
4. Always provide an option for customers to speak with a human agent if they prefer.

5. AI-Enhanced Customer Feedback Analysis
AI can help businesses make sense of large volumes of customer feedback from various sources, uncovering valuable insights.

To implement AI-driven feedback analysis in your business:
1. Aggregate feedback from multiple channels (such as reviews, social media, surveys, and customer service interactions).
2. Use an AI tool with natural language processing capabilities to analyze this data.
3. Set up a process for regularly reviewing and acting on the insights generated by the AI system.

Ethical Considerations and Best Practices

AI offers powerful tools for enhancing customer experience. However, it is critical to implement these technologies responsibly for the system to be effective. The following ethical considerations can ensure your use of AI technology follows best practices:

1. **Transparency:** Be clear with customers about when they're interacting with AI systems.

2. **Data Privacy:** Ensure compliance with data protection regulations and be transparent about data usage.
3. **Human Oversight:** Maintain human supervision of AI systems to catch and correct errors.
4. **Accessibility:** Ensure AI-driven services are accessible to all customers, including those with disabilities.
5. **Continuous Improvement:** Regularly review and update AI systems based on performance and customer feedback.
6. **Emotional Intelligence:** Train human staff to handle complex, emotionally charged situations that AI may not be equipped to manage.

The Future of AI in Customer Experience

As AI technology continues to evolve, we can expect to see the following:

1. **More Human-Like Interactions:** Advancements in NLP will make AI interactions increasingly natural and context-aware.
2. **Predictive Personalization:** AI will anticipate customer needs with increasing accuracy, enabling hyper-personalized experiences.
3. **Emotion AI:** AI systems will be able to recognize and respond to human emotions, further enhancing the customer experience.
4. **Augmented Reality (AR) Integration:** AI-powered AR experiences for product visualization and customer support will become commonplace.
5. **Seamless Omnichannel Experiences:** AI will enable more cohesive customer journeys across multiple touchpoints.

By leveraging AI to enhance customer experience, businesses can significantly improve customer satisfaction, loyalty, and, ultimately, their bottom line. The key is to implement these technologies thoughtfully, always keeping the customer's needs and preferences at the forefront. As you explore AI-driven customer experience enhancements, remember to start small, measure results, and scale successful initiatives across your business.

In the next chapter, we'll delve into how AI can optimize inventory management, a critical aspect of operations for many businesses.

Chapter 5

Optimizing Inventory Management with AI

Effective inventory management is crucial for maintaining profitability and customer satisfaction. This chapter explores how AI can transform inventory management, leading to reduced costs, improved cash flow, and better customer service.

The AI Revolution in Inventory Management

AI is reshaping inventory management in several key ways:

1. AI-Driven Demand Forecasting

Accurate demand forecasting is the foundation of effective inventory management. AI can significantly improve the accuracy of these predictions by analyzing large datasets encompassing historical sales data, market trends, and other relevant factors. This capability not only helps businesses maintain optimal inventory levels but also minimizes the risk of stockouts or excess inventory.

To implement AI-driven demand forecasting:
1. Start by consolidating historical sales data from all channels.
2. Identify external factors that influence your demand (e.g., weather, economic indicators).
3. Choose an AI forecasting tool that can integrate these various data sources.
4. Begin with forecasting for your most important product lines and gradually expand.

Remember, the quality of your forecasts will improve over time as the AI system uses more data to learn.

2. Automated Inventory Tracking and Ordering

AI can automate the process of tracking inventory levels and initiating orders when stock reaches predetermined levels. By continuously monitoring inventory data in real-time, AI-powered systems can generate accurate forecasts and trigger replenishment orders seamlessly. Overall, AI-driven inventory management not only streamlines operations but also enhances responsiveness, allowing small- and medium-sized businesses to maintain a competitive edge in today's dynamic marketplace.

To implement automated inventory tracking and ordering:

1. Ensure you have real-time inventory tracking across all locations.
2. Integrate your point-of-sale system with your inventory management system.
3. Start with automating orders for your most stable, predictable product lines.
4. Gradually increase automation as you gain confidence in the system.

3. Reducing Waste and Improving Cash Flow

AI can help businesses optimize their inventory levels to reduce waste, which is especially crucial for businesses that handle perishable goods. For example, AI can automate the monitoring of inventory freshness and quality, ensuring that items are rotated appropriately and disposed of when necessary to prevent waste. This not only improves efficiency and reduces costs but also supports sustainability initiatives by minimizing the environmental impact of your business.

To implement AI for perishable inventory management:

1. Implement detailed tracking of inventory age and condition.
2. Integrate your pricing system with your inventory management system.
3. Use AI to dynamically adjust prices as products near their expiration dates.
4. Consider implementing IoT sensors to monitor product conditions in real time.

4. Supply Chain Optimization

AI can analyze complex supply chain data to identify inefficiencies and suggest improvements. By processing vast amounts of data from various sources, such as production schedules, logistics routes, inventory levels, and supplier performance metrics, AI algorithms can uncover hidden patterns and correlations. These insights enable businesses to optimize their supply chain operations by identifying bottlenecks, reducing lead times, optimizing inventory distribution, and improving overall operational efficiency.

To implement AI for supply chain optimization:
1. Map out your entire supply chain, identifying key data points at each stage.
2. Implement systems to collect real-time data across your supply chain.
3. Use AI to analyze this data and identify patterns and potential improvements.
4. Start with optimizing one aspect of your supply chain (for example, routing) before expanding to others.

5. Multi-Location Inventory Optimization

For businesses with multiple locations or warehouses, AI can optimize inventory distribution across the network. AI algorithms can determine the optimal allocation of products in each location to minimize shipping costs, reduce delivery times, and ensure adequate stock levels. Such an intelligent distribution strategy not only enhances operational efficiency but also improves overall customer satisfaction by ensuring products are available when and where they are needed.

To implement multi-location inventory optimization:
1. Centralize inventory data from all locations.
2. Ensure you have a clear view of transfer costs between locations.
3. Use AI to analyze demand patterns across your network and optimize distribution.
4. Start with your most important product categories and expand gradually.

Challenges and Considerations

While AI offers significant benefits for inventory management, there are challenges to consider:

1. **Data Quality:** AI systems rely on accurate data. Out-of-date or corrupted data can significantly detriment your AI implementation.
2. **Integration Complexity:** Integrating AI solutions with existing systems can be technically challenging and costly.
3. **Staff Training:** Employees need to understand how to work with AI systems, requiring costly training.
4. **Initial Costs:** While AI can lead to long-term savings, there may be significant upfront costs.
5. **Overreliance on AI:** AI can miss things and will require human oversight to catch any errors.

Best Practices for AI Implementation in Inventory Management

The following process will help you streamline your AI implementation in inventory management and mitigate many of the challenges listed above:

1. **Start Small:** Begin with a pilot project in one area of inventory management before scaling.
2. **Ensure Data Readiness:** Clean and organize your data before implementing AI systems.
3. **Choose the Right Solution:** Select AI tools that integrate well with your existing systems and business processes.
4. **Set Clear Objectives:** Define specific, measurable goals for your AI implementation.
5. **Maintain Human Oversight:** While AI can automate many processes, human judgment is still crucial for strategic decisions.
6. **Continuous Improvement:** Regularly review and refine your AI models based on real-world performance.
7. **Collaborate with Suppliers:** Share relevant data and insights with suppliers to improve overall supply chain efficiency.

The Future of AI in Inventory Management

As AI technology continues to evolve, we can expect to see the following:

1. **Increased Automation:** More fully automated warehouses with AI-driven robotics.
2. **Enhanced Predictive Capabilities:** AI models that can predict and adapt to complex market changes in real time.
3. **Blockchain Integration:** Combining AI with blockchain for improved traceability and transparency in the supply chain.
4. **Sustainability Focus:** AI systems that optimize inventory not just for cost but also for environmental impact.
5. **Augmented Reality Integration:** AI-powered AR for improved picking, packing, and inventory auditing processes.

By leveraging AI for inventory management, businesses can significantly improve their operational efficiency, reduce costs, and enhance their ability to meet customer demand. As with any significant technological implementation, however, you must approach AI adoption strategically, with clear goals and a willingness to continuously learn and adapt. With the right method, AI can transform inventory management from a necessary cost into a strategic advantage for your business.

In the next chapter, we'll explore how AI is revolutionizing marketing strategies, enabling businesses to compete more effectively and reach their target audiences with unprecedented accuracy.

Chapter 6

Revolutionizing Marketing with AI

In today's digital age, effective marketing is crucial for businesses to stand out in a crowded marketplace. This chapter explores how AI can transform your marketing strategies, enabling you to compete more effectively and reach your target audience with unprecedented precision.

AI Marketing Solutions for Every Business

AI-driven marketing solutions can revolutionize your business, providing personalized strategies and unparalleled insights to drive growth and engagement. Here's how:

1. AI-Powered Market Analysis and Trend Prediction

AI can process vast amounts of data to identify market trends and consumer behavior patterns, providing valuable insights for marketing strategies. By analyzing customer interactions and preferences, AI can help businesses tailor their marketing campaigns to target the right audience with the most relevant messages. This ability not only enhances customer engagement but also improves conversion rates and ROI.

To implement AI-powered market analysis:

1. Identify key data sources relevant to your industry (e.g., social media platforms, industry publications, search trends).
2. Choose an AI tool capable of analyzing unstructured data from multiple sources.
3. Set up a process for regularly reviewing AI-generated insights and incorporating them into your marketing strategy.

4. Start with a broad trend analysis and gradually refine the system to focus on the trends most relevant to your business.

2. Personalized Marketing Campaigns

AI enables hyper-personalization of marketing efforts, allowing businesses to deliver the right message to the right person at the right time. By leveraging machine learning algorithms and predictive analytics, AI can segment audiences based on their behaviors, preferences, and past interactions. As a result, customers receive more relevant and engaging content, which enhances their overall experience and loyalty.

To implement AI-driven personalization:
1. Consolidate customer data from various touchpoints (website interactions, purchase history, email engagement, etc.).
2. Choose an AI-powered personalization platform that integrates with your existing marketing tools.
3. Start with simple personalization (such as incorporating product recommendations in emails) and gradually increase complexity.
4. Continuously test and refine your personalization strategies based on performance data.

3. Content Creation and Optimization Using AI

AI tools can assist in creating and optimizing marketing content, from social media posts to long-form articles. These tools analyze trends, keywords, and audience preferences to generate content that resonates with the target market. By automating content creation, AI ensures consistency in brand messaging and SEO optimization while saving time and resources.

To leverage AI for content creation:

1. Identify areas where content creation is time-consuming or repetitive.
2. Choose AI writing tools that align with your content needs (for example, social media posts, product descriptions, or blog posts).
3. Establish a workflow that combines AI-generated content with human editing and refinement.
4. Use AI for content optimization, including headline testing and SEO improvements.

4. Measuring and Improving Marketing ROI with AI

AI can provide deeper insights into marketing performance and automate the optimization of marketing spend. By analyzing data from various marketing channels, customer interactions, and sales outcomes, AI can identify which strategies and campaigns are most effective in driving conversions and revenue for your business.

To implement AI-driven marketing ROI optimization:
1. Ensure you have comprehensive tracking across all marketing channels.
2. Choose an AI platform capable of multi-touch attribution modeling.
3. Start by using AI to analyze historical data and identify your most effective marketing channels.
4. Gradually implement automated budget allocation, starting with a small portion of your marketing budget.

5. AI-Driven Customer Segmentation and Targeting

AI can identify complex patterns in customer data to create more accurate and actionable customer segments. By analyzing a wide range of data points, such as purchase history, browsing behavior, demographics, and social media interactions, AI algorithms can uncover hidden correlations and trends that traditional human-driven analysis might miss. As a result, AI-driven customer segmentation and targeting can help identify emerging trends and shifts in customer preferences, allowing businesses to stay agile and responsive in a constantly evolving market.

To implement AI-driven customer segmentation:
1. Consolidate customer data from various sources into a central database.
2. Use an AI tool capable of identifying patterns and creating segments based on multiple data points.
3. Start with broad segmentation and gradually refine into more specific micro-segments.
4. Continuously test and optimize your marketing approaches for each segment.

Challenges and Considerations

While AI offers significant benefits for marketing, there are challenges to consider:

1. **Data Privacy:** Complying with data protection regulations like GDPR and CCPA can take time and effort.
2. **Algorithmic Bias:** Understanding and mitigating the potential biases in AI algorithms is essential but challenging.
3. **Over-Personalization:** Balancing personalization and customer privacy is required.
4. **Integration Complexity:** Integrating AI tools with existing marketing tech stacks is more complex than many businesses expect.
5. **Skills Gap:** Upskilling may be needed in your marketing team before they can effectively use AI tools.

Best Practices for AI Implementation in Marketing

The following best practices will make your use of AI in marketing more effective.

1. **Start with Clear Objectives:** Define specific goals for your AI marketing initiatives.
2. **Ensure Data Quality:** Clean and organize your data before implementing AI systems.
3. **Choose the Right Tools:** Select AI marketing tools that integrate well with your existing systems.
4. **Maintain Human Oversight:** While AI can automate many tasks, human creativity and strategic thinking are still crucial.
5. **Test and Iterate:** Continuously test AI-driven strategies and refine them based on results.
6. **Stay Ethical:** Ensure your AI marketing practices are transparent and respect customer privacy.
7. **Educate Your Team:** Invest in training to help your marketing team effectively leverage AI tools.

The Future of AI in Marketing

As AI technology continues to evolve, we can expect to see:

1. **More Sophisticated Predictive Analytics:** AI will become even better at predicting consumer behavior and market trends.
2. **Enhanced Natural Language Generation:** AI will create more human-like, context-aware marketing content.
3. **Advanced Visual Recognition:** AI will better understand and generate visual content for marketing.
4. **Emotion AI:** Marketing systems that can recognize and respond to human emotions.
5. **Voice Search Optimization:** AI will play a crucial role in optimizing content for voice search.

By leveraging AI in marketing, businesses can significantly enhance their ability to understand and reach their target audience, compete with larger enterprises, and achieve better returns on their marketing investments. The key is to approach AI adoption strategically, always keeping your business objectives and customer needs at the forefront. With the right approach, AI can transform marketing from a cost center into a powerful driver of business growth.

In the next chapter, we'll explore how AI is revolutionizing financial management, providing deeper insights and automating complex processes for businesses of all sizes.

Chapter 7

Streamlining Financial Management through AI

Effective financial management is crucial for any business's success and growth. This chapter explores how AI is revolutionizing financial processes, providing deeper insights, reducing errors, and freeing up valuable time for strategic decision-making.

Five Ways AI Can Streamline Your Business's Financial Management

Implementing AI in your financial management processes can significantly enhance your efficiency by providing the following benefits.

1. AI Tools for Bookkeeping and Financial Reporting

AI-powered accounting software can automate many aspects of bookkeeping and financial reporting, increasing accuracy and efficiency. By automatically categorizing transactions, reconciling accounts, and generating financial statements, AI reduces the manual effort required and minimizes the risk of human error. Additionally, AI can identify discrepancies and flag potential issues for further investigation, ensuring that financial records are accurate and compliant with regulations.

To implement AI-powered bookkeeping in your own business:
1. Choose AI-enabled accounting software that integrates with your existing systems.
2. Start by automating routine tasks like transaction categorization and bank reconciliation.

3. Gradually expand to more complex tasks like financial report generation.
4. Regularly review and refine the AI's categorizations to ensure accuracy.

2. Fraud Detection and Risk Management

AI can analyze patterns in financial data to detect anomalies and potential fraud more effectively than traditional methods. By leveraging machine learning algorithms, AI systems can continuously monitor transactions and financial activities in real-time, identifying unusual patterns or behaviors that may indicate fraudulent activity. These systems can adapt to new fraud tactics over time, becoming increasingly sophisticated in their detection capabilities.

Furthermore, AI can provide detailed analytics and reports, helping your team understand the nature of detected anomalies and implement preventive measures to strengthen your financial defenses.

To implement AI for fraud detection in your business:

1. Consolidate data from various sources (such as transactions, customer information, etc.).
2. Choose an AI system capable of real-time analysis and anomaly detection.
3. Start with detecting obvious fraud patterns and gradually refine the system to catch more subtle irregularities.
4. Maintain human oversight to investigate and confirm AI-flagged suspicious activities.

3. Cash Flow Forecasting and Optimization

AI can provide more accurate cash flow predictions and suggest optimization strategies. Its predictive capability enables businesses to anticipate cash flow fluctuations and plan accordingly, ensuring sufficient liquidity to meet financial obligations and capitalize on growth opportunities.

To implement AI-powered cash flow management:
1. Ensure you have detailed historical financial data for your business.
2. Choose an AI tool that can integrate various data sources and perform predictive analytics.
3. Start with short-term cash flow forecasting and gradually extend to longer-term predictions.
4. Use AI insights to optimize payment terms, inventory management, and other factors affecting cash flow.

4. AI-Powered Financial Analysis and Decision Support

AI can analyze complex financial data to provide insights and support strategic decision-making. By processing vast amounts of data quickly and accurately, AI algorithms can identify trends, correlations, and potential opportunities or risks that may not be apparent through traditional analysis methods. Ultimately, AI enhances the accuracy and reliability of financial analysis, enabling your business to navigate uncertainties more effectively and achieve its strategic objectives with greater confidence.

To leverage AI for financial analysis:
1. Consolidate financial data from all areas of your business.
2. Choose an AI platform capable of advanced analytics and visualization.
3. Start with basic financial ratio analysis and gradually move to more complex predictive modeling.
4. Use AI insights to complement, not replace, human financial expertise in decision-making.

5. Automated Tax Preparation and Compliance

AI can simplify tax preparation and help ensure compliance with complex tax regulations. These systems can stay up-to-date with the latest tax laws and regulations, ensuring your business adheres to compliance requirements while optimizing deductions and credits. AI can also analyze financial transactions and historical data to identify potential tax savings opportunities or areas of risk, providing valuable insights for your tax planning strategies.

To implement AI for tax management:
1. Ensure your financial data is well-organized and consistently categorized.
2. Choose AI-enabled tax software that stays updated with the latest tax regulations.
3. Start with automating basic tax calculations and gradually move to more complex tax planning.
4. Maintain human oversight, especially for complex tax situations or strategic tax planning.

Challenges and Considerations

While AI offers significant benefits for financial management, it also poses some challenges:

1. **Data Security:** You will need robust security measures to protect sensitive data.
2. **Regulatory Compliance:** AI systems must comply with financial regulations and be able to adapt to rule changes.
3. **Integration with Legacy Systems:** Older financial systems may be difficult to integrate with AI tools.
4. **Overreliance on AI:** Human oversight, especially when making complex financial decisions, is essential.
5. **Cost of Implementation:** Initial costs for AI financial tools can be significant for some businesses.

Best Practices for AI Implementation in Financial Management

A crucial aspect of implementing AI in financial management is ensuring adherence to the following best practices, which will maximize efficiency, accuracy, and strategic decision-making.

1. **Start with a Clear Strategy:** Identify specific financial processes that would benefit most from AI.
2. **Ensure Data Quality:** Clean and organize financial data before implementing AI systems.
3. **Choose the Right Solutions:** Select AI tools that integrate well with your existing financial systems.
4. **Prioritize Security:** Implement robust security measures to protect sensitive financial data.
5. **Provide Adequate Training:** Ensure your finance team is well-trained in using AI tools.
6. **Maintain Human Oversight:** Keep a team of humans available for oversight, especially for strategic financial decisions.
7. **Regularly Review and Update:** Continuously monitor AI performance and update models as needed.

The Future of AI in Financial Management

As AI technology continues to evolve, we can expect to see:

1. **More Advanced Predictive Analytics:** AI will provide even more accurate financial forecasts and risk assessments.
2. **Natural Language Processing for Financial Documents:** AI will be able to extract and analyze information from complex financial documents more effectively.
3. **Blockchain Integration:** Combining AI with blockchain for more secure and transparent financial transactions.

4. **Automated Auditing:** AI will play a larger role in the auditing process, potentially reducing costs and improving accuracy.
5. **Personalized Financial Advice:** AI systems will provide more sophisticated, personalized financial recommendations for businesses.

By leveraging AI in financial management, businesses can significantly improve their financial processes, gain deeper insights, and make more informed strategic decisions. However, as with any significant technological implementation, the key is to approach AI adoption strategically, with clear goals and a commitment to ongoing learning and adaptation. With the right approach, AI can transform financial management from a necessity into a strategic advantage for your business.

In the next chapter, we'll explore how AI can foster innovation and drive growth, helping businesses compete in rapidly evolving markets.

Chapter 8

Fostering Innovation and Growth with AI

In today's rapidly evolving business landscape, innovation is crucial for survival and growth. This chapter explores how AI can be leveraged to drive innovation, identify new opportunities, and foster a culture of continuous improvement and growth.

AI Makes it Possible to Foster Innovation and Growth in Your Business

AI opens up avenues for fostering innovation and driving growth within your business in the following ways:

1. Using AI to Identify New Business Opportunities

AI can analyze vast amounts of market data to uncover trends and opportunities that humans might miss. By processing data from various sources, such as customer behavior, competitor analysis, and economic indicators, AI algorithms can identify emerging trends, shifts in consumer preferences, and potential market gaps. Therefore, AI-driven market analysis can enhance your strategic planning and decision-making.

To implement AI for opportunity identification:
1. Identify relevant data sources (e.g., social media, industry reports, customer feedback, search trends).
2. Choose an AI tool capable of processing and analyzing unstructured data from multiple sources.
3. Set up a process for regularly reviewing AI-generated insights and incorporating them into your strategic planning.

4. Start with broad trend analysis and gradually refine the system to focus on opportunities most relevant to your business.

2. AI-Driven Product Development and Improvement
AI can streamline the product development process and provide insights for continuous improvement. Doing so allows AI to optimize resource allocation, predict potential product failures or bottlenecks in production, and recommend enhancements or adjustments to meet customer expectations.

To leverage AI in product development:
1. Integrate AI tools into your product development workflow.
2. Use machine learning to analyze product performance data and customer feedback.
3. Implement AI-powered simulation tools for faster prototyping and testing.
4. Use AI to analyze market trends and competitor products for inspiration and differentiation.

3. Competitive Analysis Using AI
AI can provide deeper insights into competitor strategies and market positioning. By gaining a deeper understanding of competitor positioning and customer perceptions, you can refine your market strategies, differentiate yourself effectively, and ultimately gain a competitive edge in your industry.

To implement AI for competitive analysis:
1. Use web scraping and AI analysis tools for competitor data collection.
2. Implement natural language processing to analyze competitor communications and customer reviews.
3. Utilize predictive analytics to forecast competitor moves.
4. Integrate competitive insights into your strategic planning process.

4. Building a Culture of Innovation with AI

AI can support a culture of innovation by providing tools for idea generation, collaboration, and decision-making. Through machine learning algorithms and NLP, AI can analyze vast amounts of data to generate insights and suggest creative solutions to complex problems. AI-powered platforms facilitate collaboration by enabling teams to share ideas, feedback, and resources in real time, regardless of geographical location, enhancing teamwork and productivity.

To build an AI-supported innovation culture:
1. Implement AI-driven idea management platforms to collect and evaluate employee suggestions.
2. Use AI to analyze and categorize ideas, identifying potential synergies and novel combinations.
3. Leverage AI for scenario planning in innovation projects to assess potential outcomes and risks.
4. Integrate AI assistants into brainstorming and planning sessions to provide relevant data and inspiration.

5. AI for Business Model Innovation

AI can help you identify opportunities for business model innovation and assess potential outcomes. By simulating various scenarios and predicting outcomes, AI enables businesses to evaluate the feasibility and profitability of different strategies before implementation. This predictive capability reduces the risks associated with innovation initiatives and provides insights that inform strategic decision-making.

To leverage AI for business model innovation:
1. Use AI tools to analyze successful business models in various industries.
2. Implement machine learning for customer behavior prediction and segmentation.

3. Leverage AI for financial modeling of potential new business models.
4. Integrate AI insights into your strategic planning and pivoting decisions.

Challenges and Considerations

While AI offers significant benefits for fostering innovation and growth, there are challenges to consider:

1. **Data Quality and Quantity:** AI systems require substantial, high-quality data to provide accurate insights.
2. **Balancing AI and Human Creativity:** While AI can provide valuable insights, human creativity and intuition remain crucial for true innovation.
3. **Ethical Considerations:** AI-driven innovations must align with ethical standards and societal values.
4. **Implementation Costs:** AI tools and training can have a significant cost for some small and medium businesses.
5. **Resistance to Change:** Employees may resist the adoption of AI tools, fearing job displacement.

Best Practices for Leveraging AI in Innovation and Growth

Using best practices ensures that AI is effectively harnessed to drive innovation and foster growth within your business.

1. **Start with Clear Objectives:** Define specific goals for your AI-driven innovation initiatives.
2. **Foster a Data-Driven Culture:** Encourage data collection and analysis across all business functions.
3. **Combine AI Insights with Human Expertise:** Use AI as a tool to augment, not replace, human creativity and decision-making.

4. **Invest in AI Education:** Provide training to help your team understand and effectively use AI tools for innovation.
5. **Embrace Experimentation:** Use AI to run more experiments and pilots, learning quickly from both successes and failures.
6. **Stay Agile:** Be prepared to pivot your strategies based on AI-driven insights and changing market conditions.
7. **Prioritize Ethical Innovation:** Ensure your AI-driven innovations align with your company's values and ethical standards.

The Future of AI in Innovation and Growth

As AI technology continues to evolve, we can expect to see:

1. **More Sophisticated Predictive Models:** AI will provide even more accurate predictions of market trends and innovation success.
2. **Advanced Natural Language Generation:** AI will assist in creating more innovative ideas and content.
3. **Autonomous Innovation Systems:** AI systems that can independently identify opportunities and suggest innovations.
4. **Quantum Computing Integration:** Quantum AI could solve complex problems and drive breakthrough innovations.
5. **AI-Human Collaborative Systems:** More advanced systems that seamlessly blend AI capabilities with human creativity.

By leveraging AI for innovation and growth, businesses can stay ahead of market trends, develop more successful products and services, and continuously evolve their business models. The key is to approach AI as a powerful tool that enhances, rather than replaces, human creativity and strategic thinking. Thus, AI can become a catalyst for ongoing innovation and sustainable growth in your business.

In the next chapter, we'll explore how AI can improve efficiency and productivity across various business operations.

Chapter 9

Improving Efficiency and Productivity with AI

In today's competitive business environment, maximizing efficiency and productivity is crucial for success. This chapter explores how AI can be leveraged to streamline operations, boost productivity, and create a more efficient work environment.

Efficiency and Productivity Benefits of AI

Here are a few ways to consider using AI to enhance your business's efficiency and productivity.

1. Measuring the Impact of AI on Business Efficiency

Before implementing AI solutions, it's important to establish baseline metrics and set clear goals for improvement. Establishing clear, achievable goals ensures that AI initiatives are aligned with your overall business objectives. Additionally, having defined metrics and goals helps in securing stakeholder buy-in and allocating resources effectively, ensuring that AI projects are well-supported and have a higher likelihood of success.

To effectively measure AI impact:
1. Conduct a thorough audit of current processes and efficiency levels.
2. Establish clear, measurable Key Performance Indicators (KPIs) for each area where AI will be implemented.
3. Implement tools to track these KPIs consistently over time.
4. Regularly review and analyze the data to assess AI's impact and identify areas for further improvement.

2. AI-Powered Project Management and Workflow Optimization

AI can significantly enhance project management and optimize workflows, leading to smoother operations and faster project completion. By leveraging AI-powered tools, project managers can automate routine tasks such as scheduling, resource allocation, and progress tracking. These tools can analyze historical project data to predict potential bottlenecks and recommend solutions, ensuring that projects stay on track and within budget.

To implement AI-powered project management:
1. Choose an AI-enabled project management tool that integrates with your existing systems.
2. Start by using AI for task assignment and scheduling optimization.
3. Gradually expand to more complex functions like risk prediction and resource allocation.
4. Train your team on how to use and interpret AI-generated insights effectively.

3. Employee Productivity Tools Driven by AI

AI can provide personalized assistance to employees, helping them work more efficiently and focus on high-value tasks. By automating repetitive and time-consuming activities such as data entry, scheduling, and routine customer inquiries, AI frees up employees to concentrate on more strategic and creative work.

To leverage AI for employee productivity:
1. Identify repetitive, time-consuming tasks that could be automated or optimized with AI.
2. Choose AI productivity tools that integrate well with your existing systems and workflows.
3. Start with simple applications like email management or meeting scheduling, then expand to more complex tasks.

4. Provide comprehensive training to ensure employees can fully utilize the AI tools.

4. AI for Process Automation and Optimization

AI can identify inefficiencies in business processes and suggest or implement improvements. Machine learning algorithms can process data from various sources, such as workflow logs, employee activity, and system performance metrics, to pinpoint areas where resources are being underutilized, or processes are slowing down. Once identified, AI can provide actionable insights and recommendations for streamlining these processes, such as automating repetitive tasks, reallocating resources, or optimizing workflows.

To implement AI for process optimization:
1. Conduct a thorough audit of current processes to identify potential areas for improvement.
2. Implement sensors or data collection methods to gather relevant process data.
3. Choose an AI system capable of analyzing this data and generating actionable insights.
4. Start with optimizing one specific process and gradually expand to others as you see results.

5. AI-Enhanced Decision-Making for Improved Efficiency

AI can provide data-driven insights to support faster, more accurate decision-making. These insights enable businesses to make informed decisions based on empirical evidence rather than intuition or guesswork.

To implement AI-enhanced decision-making:
1. Identify key decision points in your business where data-driven insights could be valuable.

2. Ensure you have systems in place to collect relevant data for these decision points.
3. Implement AI analytics tools that can process this data and generate actionable insights.
4. Start by using AI to inform decisions in one area of your business, then expand as you see positive results.

Challenges and Considerations

While AI offers significant benefits for improving efficiency and productivity, there are challenges to consider:

1. **Initial Productivity Dip:** There may be a temporary decrease in productivity as employees learn new AI-driven systems.
2. **Over-reliance on AI:** Critical thinking and human judgment may be overlooked in favor of AI recommendations.
3. **Data Privacy and Security:** AI often involves handling sensitive data, which can be breached without robust security measures.
4. **Employee Concerns:** Fears about job displacement can harm team productivity and the workplace atmosphere.
5. **Integration Complexity:** Seamless integration of AI tools with existing systems can be challenging.

Best Practices for AI Implementation in Efficiency and Productivity

Implementing AI effectively requires adherence to the following best practices that ensure seamless integration and optimal performance.

1. **Start with a Clear Strategy:** Identify specific processes and areas where AI can have the most significant impact.

2. **Ensure Data Quality:** Clean and organize your data before implementing AI systems.
3. **Prioritize User Experience:** Choose AI tools with intuitive interfaces to encourage adoption.
4. **Provide Comprehensive Training:** Ensure all employees are well-trained in using new AI tools.
5. **Encourage Feedback:** Create channels for employees to provide feedback on AI tools and suggest improvements.
6. **Monitor and Adjust:** Continuously track the impact of AI on efficiency and productivity, adjusting strategies as needed.
7. **Balance AI and Human Skills:** Use AI to augment human capabilities rather than replace them entirely.

The Future of AI in Efficiency and Productivity

As AI technology continues to evolve, we can expect to see:

1. **More Advanced Predictive Capabilities:** AI will provide even more accurate predictions for process optimization and resource allocation.
2. **Enhanced NLP:** Improved AI assistants that can handle more complex tasks and interactions.
3. **Augmented Reality Integration:** AI-powered AR for hands-free guidance in various tasks, improving efficiency in fields like manufacturing and maintenance.
4. **Emotional Intelligence in AI:** AI systems that can recognize and respond to human emotions, improving workplace dynamics and productivity.
5. **Autonomous Systems:** More advanced AI systems that can manage entire processes with minimal human intervention.

By leveraging AI to improve efficiency and productivity, businesses can significantly enhance their competitiveness and profitability. The key is to approach AI implementation strategically, with a focus on empowering employees and optimizing processes rather than simply replacing human tasks. With the right approach, AI can become a powerful tool for creating a more efficient, productive, and innovative work environment.

In the next chapter, we'll explore the critical topic of enhancing employee skills for the AI era, ensuring your workforce is prepared to thrive in an AI-augmented workplace.

Chapter 10

Enhancing Employee Skills for the AI Era

As AI becomes increasingly integrated into business operations, you must ensure your workforce is equipped with the skills needed to thrive in this new environment. This chapter explores strategies for identifying key AI skills, implementing effective training programs, and building an AI-savvy workforce.

Helping Your Employees Prepare for the AI Era

Preparing your employees for the AI era is crucial to ensuring a smooth transition and maximizing the benefits of AI integration within your organization.

1. Identifying Key AI Skills for Your Employees

Understanding the essential skills needed to work effectively with AI is the first step in preparing your workforce for the AI era. Training programs should focus on both technical and soft skills, ensuring employees are proficient in areas such as data analysis, machine learning basics, and AI tool usage. Providing hands-on experience with AI applications through workshops and real-world projects can further enhance their confidence and competence. By investing in comprehensive training and development, businesses can empower their employees to harness AI's full potential, driving innovation and maintaining a competitive edge in the evolving market landscape.

To conduct your own AI skills assessment:
1.   Define the AI skills relevant to your business (for example., data analysis, machine learning basics, and AI ethics).

2. Develop assessment tools to evaluate these skills among your employees.
3. Analyze the results to identify skill gaps and areas of strength.
4. Use these insights to inform your training and hiring strategies.

2. Core AI Skills for the Modern Workforce

Core AI skills are increasingly essential for the modern workforce to thrive in an AI-driven environment. Ensure that your employees are equipped with the following skills before implementing AI initiatives in your business.

1. **Data Literacy:** The ability to read, understand, create, and communicate data as information.
2. **Basic AI and Machine Learning Concepts:** Understanding how AI works and its potential applications.
3. **AI Ethics and Responsible Use:** Awareness of ethical considerations in AI implementation and use.
4. **Problem-Solving with AI:** The ability to identify where and how AI can be applied to business challenges.
5. **AI-Human Collaboration:** The skills needed to work alongside AI systems effectively.

3. Strategies for AI Training and Upskilling

Developing a comprehensive AI training program is crucial for building an AI-savvy workforce. Such a program should begin with foundational courses that introduce employees to basic AI concepts, terminology, and applications relevant to their roles. By investing in comprehensive AI training, organizations can equip their workforce with the skills and knowledge necessary to harness AI's transformative potential, driving innovation, efficiency, and competitive advantage in the digital age.

To develop an effective AI training program:

1. Create a multi-tiered training structure (e.g., AI awareness, AI basics, advanced AI skills).
2. Utilize a mix of training methods (such as online courses, workshops, mentoring, and hands-on projects).
3. Partner with educational institutions or AI vendors for specialized training.
4. Implement a continuous learning model to keep pace with AI advancements.
5. Offer incentives for completing AI training and applying new skills.

4. Building an AI-Savvy Culture

Creating a culture that embraces AI and encourages continuous learning is key to building an AI-savvy workforce. This process involves fostering an environment where employees feel empowered to experiment with new technologies and are supported in their efforts to acquire new skills. Additionally, encouraging collaboration and knowledge sharing among team members can facilitate the integration of AI into various business processes.

To build an AI-savvy culture:
1. **Lead by example:** Ensure leadership is actively engaged in AI learning and application.
2. **Encourage experimentation:** Create safe spaces for employees to test AI applications.
3. **Recognize and reward AI initiatives:** Highlight successful AI projects and innovations.
4. **Foster cross-departmental AI collaboration:** Create opportunities for knowledge sharing.
5. **Integrate AI into your company's mission and values:** Embed AI goals into strategic planning, promote ethical standards and transparency, and communicate AI's role in achieving long-term objectives.

5. Managing the Human-AI Collaboration

Preparing employees to work effectively alongside AI is crucial for maximizing the benefits of AI adoption. Employees should be encouraged to develop a growth mindset, seeing AI as a tool that can enhance their capabilities rather than a threat to their jobs.

To foster effective human-AI collaboration:

1. Clearly define roles and responsibilities for humans and AI in various processes.
2. Train employees on how to interpret and act on AI-generated insights.
3. Emphasize the importance of human judgment in AI-assisted decision-making.
4. Develop protocols for handling AI errors or unexpected outputs.
5. Regularly review and optimize human-AI workflows.

Challenges and Considerations

While enhancing employee skills for the AI era is crucial, there are challenges to consider:

1. **Rapid Pace of AI Advancement:** Keeping training current with fast-evolving AI technology can be challenging.
2. **Varied Learning Curves:** Employees may adapt to AI at different rates, requiring flexible training approaches.
3. **Balancing Training and Productivity:** Finding time for AI training without disrupting daily operations can be difficult.
4. **Measuring ROI on AI Training:** Quantifying the impact of AI skills enhancement on business outcomes can be complex.
5. **Addressing Job Security Concerns:** Some employees may resist AI training due to fears about job displacement.

Best Practices for Enhancing Employee Skills in the AI Era

Implementing the following best practices for enhancing employee skills in the AI era is crucial.

1. **Tailor Training to Business Needs:** Align AI skill development with your specific business goals and challenges.
2. **Make Learning Continuous:** Implement ongoing learning programs rather than one-off training sessions.
3. **Emphasize Practical Application:** Focus on how AI skills can be applied to real-world business problems.
4. **Foster a Supportive Learning Environment:** Encourage experimentation and learning from mistakes in AI use.
5. **Collaborate with AI Experts:** Partner with AI vendors, academic institutions, or consultants for specialized training.
6. **Monitor and Adapt:** Regularly assess the effectiveness of your AI training programs and adjust as needed.

The Future of AI Skills in the Workplace

As AI continues to evolve, we can expect to see:

1. **Increased Demand for AI-Human Interaction Skills:** The ability to effectively collaborate with AI systems will become increasingly valuable.
2. **Growing Importance of AI Ethics:** Understanding and applying ethical considerations in AI use will be crucial.
3. **Rise of AI Specializations:** More specialized AI roles and skills will emerge across various business functions.
4. **Continuous Learning as the Norm:** Regular upskilling in AI will become an expected part of most jobs.

5. **AI Literacy as a Basic Skill:** Understanding AI fundamentals will become as essential as digital literacy is today.

By prioritizing the development of AI skills among employees, your business can create a workforce that is not only prepared for the AI era but can also drive innovation and competitive advantage through effective AI use. The key is to approach AI skill development as an ongoing journey, continuously adapting to new technologies and finding ways to augment human capabilities with AI.

In the next chapter, we'll explore strategies for investing in AI, including budgeting considerations and how to scale AI usage as your business grows.

Chapter 11

Investing in AI: Strategies for Your Business

For many businesses, investing in AI can seem daunting due to perceived high costs and complexity. However, with the right approach, AI investment can be both affordable and highly rewarding. This chapter explores strategies for businesses to invest in AI effectively, from budgeting to scaling AI usage as your business grows.

Tips for Using AI Strategically

Employing AI strategically requires a thoughtful approach to integration, ensuring that it aligns with your organization's goals and enhances overall efficiency and innovation. The following tips will help.

1. Budgeting for AI Adoption

Developing a realistic and effective budget for AI adoption is crucial for businesses with limited resources. It is important to prioritize investments in scalable solutions that offer the best return on investment. By carefully planning and managing the budget, businesses can implement AI solutions that drive growth and efficiency without overstretching their financial limits.

Key considerations for AI budgeting:
1. Initial costs (software, hardware, data preparation).
2. Ongoing expenses (subscriptions, maintenance, updates).
3. Training and upskilling costs.
4. Potential savings and revenue increases from AI implementation.

To develop an effective AI budget:
1. Start with a thorough assessment of your current technology infrastructure and data readiness.
2. Identify specific business problems that AI could address and estimate the potential value of solving them.
3. Research various AI solutions, including cloud-based services, to understand the range of costs.
4. Allocate funds for employee training and change management.
5. Build in a buffer for unexpected costs or necessary pivots.
6. Plan for both short-term investments and long-term scalability.

2. Choosing the Right AI Solutions for Your Business

Selecting appropriate AI solutions is critical for maximizing the return on your AI investment. It is essential to evaluate different AI technologies and platforms to determine which ones best align with your needs and goals. By making informed and strategic choices, your business can leverage AI to drive significant improvements in efficiency, productivity, and innovation.

To choose the right AI solutions:
1. Conduct a thorough needs assessment across all departments.
2. Prioritize areas where AI can have the most significant impact on your business goals.
3. Consider both off-the-shelf solutions and custom development options.
4. Evaluate potential AI vendors based on their expertise, support, and alignment with your business needs.
5. Ensure the chosen solutions can integrate with your existing systems.
6. Start with a pilot project to test the solution before full-scale implementation.

3. ROI Considerations for AI Investments

Understanding and measuring the return on investment is crucial for justifying AI expenditures and guiding future investments. This effort involves setting clear, measurable objectives for AI initiatives from the outset, such as increased efficiency, cost savings, revenue growth, or improved customer satisfaction. Additionally, comparing the costs associated with AI implementation (including hardware, software, training, and maintenance) against the tangible and intangible benefits can provide a comprehensive view of ROI.

Key metrics to consider when measuring AI ROI:

1. Cost savings (e.g., reduced labor costs, improved efficiency).
2. Revenue increases (e.g., higher sales through personalization).
3. Customer satisfaction and retention improvements.
4. Error reduction and quality improvements.
5. Time saved on manual tasks.
6. New revenue streams enabled by AI.

To effectively measure AI ROI:

1. Establish clear baseline metrics before AI implementation.
2. Set specific, measurable goals for each AI initiative.
3. Track both direct financial impacts and indirect benefits.
4. Consider long-term value creation, not just short-term gains.
5. Regularly review and adjust your AI investments based on ROI data.

4. Scaling AI Usage as Your Business Grows

As businesses experience success with initial AI implementations, it's important to have a strategy for scaling AI usage. Investing in scalable AI infrastructure and tools that can handle increased workloads is essential for smooth expansion. Regularly reviewing and refining the AI strategy based on feedback and performance metrics can also ensure that the scaling efforts remain aligned with your business's goals.

Strategies for scaling AI usage:
1. Create an AI roadmap that aligns with your overall business strategy.
2. Gradually expand AI use cases across different departments.
3. Develop internal AI expertise through hiring and training.
4. Establish an AI governance framework to ensure responsible and consistent AI use.
5. Continuously monitor AI performance and gather feedback for improvements.
6. Be prepared to upgrade your data infrastructure to support more advanced AI applications.

Challenges and Considerations

While investing in AI offers significant potential benefits, businesses should be aware of potential challenges:

1. **Data Quality and Quantity:** Ensuring sufficient high-quality data for AI systems can be challenging for smaller businesses.
2. **Integration Complexities:** Integrating AI solutions with existing legacy systems can be technically challenging and costly.
3. **Skill Gaps:** Finding or developing employees with the right AI skills can be difficult in a competitive market.
4. **Keeping Pace with AI Advancements:** Keeping pace with the rapid evolution of AI technology can be challenging.

5. **Ethical and Regulatory Compliance:** Navigating the ethical implications and regulatory requirements of AI use can be complex.

Best Practices for AI Investment

Adopting the following best practices for AI investment is essential to ensure that resources are allocated effectively, maximizing the impact and return on AI initiatives.

1. **Align AI Investments with Business Strategy:** Ensure AI initiatives support core business objectives.
2. **Start Small and Scale:** Begin with pilot projects and scale based on proven success.
3. **Prioritize Data Readiness:** Invest in data collection, cleaning, and management alongside AI tools.
4. **Foster Cross-Functional Collaboration:** Involve multiple departments in AI planning and implementation.
5. **Invest in Employee Development:** Allocate resources for ongoing AI training and upskilling.
6. **Stay Agile:** Be prepared to pivot your AI strategy based on results and changing business needs.
7. **Consider Partnerships:** Explore partnerships with AI vendors, startups, or academic institutions to access expertise and resources.

The Future of AI Investment

As AI technology continues to evolve, we can expect to see:

1. **More Accessible AI Solutions:** Increasing availability of affordable, SMB-focused AI tools and platforms.
2. **AI-as-a-Service Models:** Growing subscription-based AI services will reduce upfront investment needs.
3. **Industry-Specific AI Solutions:** Expanding AI tools will be tailored to specific industries and business needs.

4. **Increased Focus on Explainable AI:** Growing demand for AI systems that can clearly explain their decision-making processes.
5. **AI Marketplaces:** Emergence of marketplaces where businesses can easily find and implement AI solutions.

By approaching AI investment strategically, businesses can leverage the power of AI to drive growth, improve efficiency, and compete more effectively in their markets. The key is to start with clear objectives, choose solutions carefully, and be prepared to adapt and scale as your business and AI capabilities grow. With thoughtful investment and implementation, AI can become a powerful driver of success for businesses of all sizes.

In the next chapter, we'll explore how smaller businesses can use AI to compete effectively with larger enterprises, leveling the playing field in various industries.

Chapter 12

Competing with Larger Enterprises Using AI

One of the most significant advantages AI offers smaller businesses is the ability to level the playing field with larger competitors. This chapter explores how your small or medium business can leverage AI to punch above its weight, compete effectively with larger enterprises, and carve out unique market positions.

Leveling the Playing Field with AI Capabilities

AI can provide smaller businesses with capabilities that were once only available to large enterprises with substantial resources. By leveraging AI, small businesses can automate routine tasks, enhance customer service with chatbots, and gain valuable insights from data analytics. This democratization of technology allows smaller companies to compete on a more level playing field, improving their efficiency and decision-making processes. Moreover, affordable AI tools and platforms are now more accessible, enabling small businesses to implement solutions that drive innovation and growth without the need for significant capital investment.

To implement similar AI capabilities:
1. Start by consolidating your customer data from various sources.
2. Choose AI tools that specialize in your specific needs (for example, personalization, and inventory management).
3. Focus on areas where you can differentiate yourself from larger competitors.

4. Leverage cloud-based AI services to access advanced capabilities without large upfront investments.

Strategies for Smaller Businesses to Outmaneuver Larger Competitors

Smaller businesses can use AI to create strategic advantages that allow them to outperform larger, less agile competitors. By swiftly adopting AI-driven solutions, they can enhance their operational efficiency, personalize customer interactions, and make data-driven decisions that larger organizations may struggle to implement quickly. This agility and responsiveness give smaller businesses a competitive edge, enabling them to tailor their products and services more precisely to customer needs and stay ahead in a dynamic market landscape.

Key strategies for outmaneuvering larger competitors:
1. Rapid innovation and market responsiveness.
2. Hyper-personalization of products and services.
3. Niche market focus with deep AI-driven insights.
4. Agile decision-making powered by real-time AI analytics.

To implement these strategies:
1. Use AI for rapid prototyping and market testing of new ideas.
2. Leverage AI to gain deep insights into niche markets.
3. Implement AI-driven decision-making tools to increase agility.
4. Focus on areas where larger competitors are slow to adapt.

Real-World Examples of Smaller Businesses Successfully Competing Against Larger Firms

1. Stitch Fix, an online personal styling service:

Challenge: Competing with national chains and e-commerce giants
AI Solution: Implemented AI chatbot for product recommendations
Results:
- 100% of customers receive AI-powered recommendations.
- Over 4.5 billion textual data points from customers.[4]
- 77% pass rate for AI-generated copy.

2. FC Beauty, a Dubai-based skincare company:

Challenge: Competing with large, international brands
AI Solution: Implemented AI-driven predictive analytics for inventory management[5]
Results:
- AI algorithms provided precise demand forecasts, reducing the risk of overstock.
- Achieved an 8% reduction in excess stock within two months of implementation.
- A 15% increase in sales by ensuring product availability

3. Allcasting, a casting agency for models and artists:

Challenge: Competing with large, established agencies
AI Solution: Used AI to find talent and hold auditions
Results:

---

[4] Bernard Marr, "How Stitch Fix Is Using Generative AI To Help Us Dress Better," *Forbes*, March 8, 2024, accessed July 17, 2024, https://www.forbes.com/sites/bernardmarr/2024/03/08/how-stitch-fix-is-using-generative-ai-to-help-us-dress-better/.

[5] Georgia Lewis, "How four small businesses are getting a bang for their AI buck," Raconteur.net, Feburary 23, 2024, accessed July 17, 2024, https://www.raconteur.net/technology/four-ai-case-studies.

- Increased diversity of talent.[6]
- Improved efficiency.
- Boosted box office success.

Future Trends in AI that May Benefit Smaller Businesses

As AI technology evolves, new opportunities for smaller businesses to gain competitive advantages are emerging:

1. **Explainable AI (XAI):**
   Benefit: Allows smaller businesses to build trust with customers by providing transparent AI-driven decisions.
   Example: A small financial advisory firm using XAI to explain investment recommendations, competing with larger, less transparent robo-advisors.

2. **Edge AI:**
   Benefit: Enables AI processing on local devices, reducing costs and improving speed.
   Example: A small retailer using edge AI for real-time inventory management and customer tracking, matching the in-store experience of larger chains.

3. **AI-Powered Augmented and Virtual Reality:**
   Benefit: Enables immersive customer experiences without large physical infrastructure.
   Example: A small furniture store using AI-powered AR to allow customers to visualize products in their homes, competing with larger showrooms.

4. **Federated Learning:**

---

[6] Matt Sheils, "The Future of Casting and Actor Selection with AI," Mattsheils.com, accessed July 17, 2024, https://www.mattsheils.com/blog/the-future-of-casting-and-actor-selection-with-ai.

Benefit: Allows AI models to be trained across multiple decentralized devices, preserving data privacy.
Example: A small healthcare provider collaborating with others to train AI diagnostic tools without sharing sensitive patient data.

5. **AutoML (Automated Machine Learning):**
   Benefit: Simplifies the process of developing ML models, making AI more accessible to smaller businesses.
   Example: A small marketing agency is using AutoML to develop sophisticated customer segmentation models that rival the capabilities of larger agencies.

Challenges and Considerations

While AI offers significant competitive advantages, smaller businesses should be aware of potential challenges:

1. **Data Limitations:** Smaller businesses may have less data than larger competitors, potentially impacting AI effectiveness.
2. **Resource Constraints:** Limited budgets and expertise can make it challenging to implement and maintain advanced AI systems.
3. **Keeping Pace with AI Advancements:** The rapid evolution of AI technology requires ongoing learning and adaptation.
4. **Ethical and Regulatory Compliance:** The ethical implications and regulatory requirements of AI use can be complex to navigate.
5. **Cybersecurity Risks:** AI may introduce new security vulnerabilities that need to be addressed during implementation.

Best Practices for Smaller Businesses Competing with AI

Implementing the following best practices for smaller businesses competing with AI is essential to harness the technology's full potential and maintain a competitive edge in the market.

1. **Focus on Niche Excellence:** Use AI to become the absolute best in a specific niche or market segment.
2. **Emphasize Agility:** Leverage your smaller size to implement and iterate on AI solutions faster than larger competitors.
3. **Collaborate and Partner:** Form partnerships or join AI consortiums to access larger datasets and shared resources.
4. **Prioritize Customer-Centric AI:** Focus on AI applications that directly enhance customer experience and value.
5. **Invest in AI Education:** Ensure your team is continuously learning about AI to maintain a competitive edge.
6. **Start Small, Think Big:** Begin with focused AI projects, but develop a long-term AI strategy for sustained competition.
7. **Highlight Your AI Advantage:** Make your AI capabilities a key part of your marketing and differentiation strategy.

By strategically leveraging AI, smaller businesses can not only compete with larger enterprises but also carve out unique market positions that larger companies may struggle to match. The key is to focus on areas where AI can amplify your existing strengths, address critical market needs, and provide exceptional value to your customers. With the right approach, AI can be a powerful equalizer, enabling businesses of all sizes to thrive in even the most competitive markets.

In the next chapter, we'll explore how AI is transforming data analytics and decision-making processes, enabling businesses to harness the power of their data more effectively than ever before.

Chapter 13

Data Analytics and Decision-Making with AI

In the era of big data, the ability to extract meaningful insights and make data-driven decisions is crucial for businesses to remain competitive. This chapter explores how AI is revolutionizing data analytics and decision-making processes, enabling businesses to harness the power of their data more effectively than ever before.

Understanding the Basics of AI-Driven Data Analytics

AI-powered data analytics goes beyond traditional methods, offering deeper insights and predictive capabilities.

Key components of AI-driven analytics:
1. **Machine Learning** algorithms for pattern recognition and prediction.
2. **Natural Language Processing** for analyzing text data.
3. **Computer Vision** for image and video analysis.
4. **Deep Learning** for complex, multi-layered data analysis.

Benefits for businesses:
1. Ability to process and analyze large volumes of data quickly.
2. Uncovering hidden patterns and correlations.
3. More accurate predictions and forecasts.
4. Real-time analysis and insights.

To implement AI-driven analytics:

1. Assess your current data infrastructure and identify areas for improvement.
2. Choose AI analytics tools that align with your specific business needs.
3. Ensure you have clean, high-quality data to feed into your AI systems.
4. Start with a specific business problem and expand as you see results.

Implementing Data-Driven Decision-Making in Your Business

Transitioning to a data-driven decision-making culture is crucial for leveraging the full potential of AI analytics.

Key steps to implement data-driven decision-making:
1. Establish a data-centric culture across the organization.
2. Invest in AI tools and platforms for data analysis.
3. Train employees on data interpretation and AI-assisted decision-making.
4. Create processes for incorporating data insights into decision-making workflows.
5. Regularly review and refine your data-driven strategies.

To foster a data-driven culture:
1. Lead by example and ensure leadership uses data in their decision-making processes.
2. Provide easy access to relevant data and insights for all employees.
3. Encourage experimentation and learning from data-driven decisions.
4. Recognize and reward data-driven successes.

Overcoming Data Challenges in Smaller Businesses

Smaller businesses often face unique challenges when it comes to implementing AI-driven data analytics. Here are some common challenges and solutions to consider before adopting AI technology.

Common challenges and solutions:

1. **Limited data volume:**
   Solution: Leverage external data sources, industry benchmarks, and partnerships.

2. **Data quality issues:**
   Solution: Implement data cleaning and validation processes and invest in data management tools.

3. **Lack of data expertise:**
   Solution: Provide training for existing staff, consider hiring a data specialist, or partner with data analytics firms.

4. **Budget constraints:**
   Solution: Start with cloud-based AI analytics tools, which often have lower upfront costs.

AI-Powered Predictive Analytics for Businesses

Predictive analytics is one of the most powerful applications of AI in data analysis. It allows businesses to anticipate future trends and behaviors. This foresight enables companies to make proactive decisions, optimize operations, and tailor marketing strategies to meet customer needs more effectively. Overall, predictive analytics empowers small and medium organizations to stay ahead of the curve and maintain a competitive advantage in an ever-evolving market.

Key applications of predictive analytics:
1. Sales forecasting.
2. Customer churn prediction.
3. Inventory optimization.
4. Risk assessment.
5. Maintenance scheduling.

To implement predictive analytics:
1. Identify specific business problems that could benefit from predictive insights.
2. Ensure you have historical data relevant to these problems.
3. Choose AI tools specifically designed for predictive analytics.
4. Start with a pilot project to demonstrate value before scaling up.

Ethical Considerations in AI-Driven Data Analytics

As businesses embrace AI for data analytics, it's crucial to consider the ethical implications.

Key ethical concerns in AI-driven analytics:
1. Data privacy and security.
2. Algorithmic bias and fairness.
3. Transparency and explainability of AI decisions.
4. Responsible use of predictive insights.

Best practices for ethical AI in data analytics:
1. Implement robust data protection measures.
2. Regularly audit AI systems for bias.
3. Ensure transparency in how AI insights are generated and used.
4. Establish clear guidelines for ethical AI use in your organization.

5. Provide mechanisms for stakeholders to challenge or appeal AI-driven decisions.

The Future of AI in Data Analytics and Decision-Making

As AI technology continues to evolve, we can expect to see:

1. **Automated Data Scientists:** AI systems that can perform complex data analysis tasks with minimal human intervention.
2. **Enhanced Natural Language Interfaces:** The ability to query data and receive insights using conversational language.
3. **Real-Time Decision Making:** AI systems that can make and implement decisions in real-time based on streaming data.
4. **Augmented Analytics:** AI-powered tools that guide users through the entire analytics workflow, from data preparation to insight generation.
5. **Edge Analytics:** The ability to perform advanced analytics on IoT devices, enabling faster decision-making at the point of data collection.

Businesses can gain a significant competitive advantage by leveraging AI for data analytics and decision-making. The key is to approach AI implementation strategically, focusing on specific business problems and gradually building your capabilities. With the right approach, AI can transform your business into a data-driven powerhouse capable of making faster, more accurate decisions that drive growth and innovation.

In the next chapter, we'll explore the critical topic of AI ethics and governance and how businesses can ensure the responsible and trustworthy use of AI technologies.

5. Provide mechanisms for stakeholders to challenge or appeal AI-driven decisions.

The Future of AI in Data Analytics and Decision-Making

As AI technology continues to evolve, we can expect to see:

1. **Automated Data Scientists:** AI systems that can perform complex data analysis tasks with minimal human intervention.
2. **Enhanced Natural Language Interfaces:** The ability to query data and receive insights using conversational language.
3. **Real-Time Decision Making:** AI systems that can make and implement decisions in real-time based on streaming data.
4. **Augmented Analytics:** AI-powered tools that guide users through the entire analytics workflow, from data preparation to insight generation.
5. **Edge Analytics:** The ability to perform advanced analytics on IoT devices, enabling faster decision-making at the point of data collection.

Businesses can gain a significant competitive advantage by leveraging AI for data analytics and decision-making. The key is to approach AI implementation strategically, focusing on specific business problems and gradually building your capabilities. With the right approach, AI can transform your business into a data-driven powerhouse capable of making faster, more accurate decisions that drive growth and innovation.

In the next chapter, we'll explore the critical topic of AI ethics and governance and how businesses can ensure the responsible and trustworthy use of AI technologies.

Chapter 14

Ethical Considerations and AI Governance for Businesses

As businesses increasingly adopt AI technologies, it's crucial to address the ethical implications and establish proper governance frameworks. This chapter explores the key ethical considerations surrounding AI use and provides guidance on implementing responsible AI practices.

Understanding AI Ethics and Its Importance for Businesses

AI ethics refers to the moral principles and guidelines that govern the development and use of artificial intelligence technologies. As AI technologies become more integrated into various aspects of daily life, addressing ethical concerns becomes increasingly critical to ensure that AI benefits society as a whole while minimizing potential risks and drawbacks.

Key ethical considerations:
1. Fairness and non-discrimination.
2. Transparency and explainability.
3. Privacy and data protection.
4. Accountability and responsibility.
5. Safety and security.

Importance for businesses:
1. Building trust with customers and stakeholders.
2. Mitigating risks associated with AI use.
3. Ensuring compliance with emerging AI regulations.
4. Enhancing brand reputation.
5. Fostering innovation within ethical boundaries.

Developing an AI Ethics Framework for Your Business

Creating a comprehensive AI ethics framework is crucial for guiding the responsible use of AI in your business. This framework should outline clear principles and guidelines that align with your company's values and ethical standards. Regularly reviewing and updating the AI ethics framework in response to technological advancements and societal changes also helps ensure continued alignment with best practices and regulatory requirements.

Key components of an AI ethics framework:
1. Clear ethical principles and values.
2. Guidelines for responsible AI development and use.
3. Processes for ethical review of AI projects.
4. Training programs on AI ethics for employees.
5. Mechanisms for addressing ethical concerns and violations.

To develop your AI ethics framework:
1. Engage stakeholders from across your organization in the development process.
2. Research existing AI ethics frameworks and adapt them to your business context.
3. Clearly define roles and responsibilities for AI ethics within your organization.
4. Create processes for ongoing monitoring and updating of the framework.
5. Integrate ethical considerations into your AI development and deployment workflows.

Ensuring Data Privacy and Security with AI

As AI systems often rely on large amounts of data, ensuring privacy and security is paramount. By prioritizing privacy and security measures, your business can mitigate potential risks associated with AI technologies and foster confidence among users in its responsible handling of data.

Key considerations for data privacy and security:
1. Data minimization and purpose limitation.
2. Anonymization and pseudonymization techniques.
3. Secure data storage and transmission.
4. Access controls and authentication measures.
5. Regular security audits and updates.

Best practices:
1. Implement robust data protection policies and procedures.
2. Use encryption for data at rest and in transit.
3. Regularly train employees on data privacy and security best practices.
4. Conduct regular risk assessments and penetration testing.
5. Be transparent with customers about data usage and AI applications.

Building Trust with Customers and Employees Through Responsible AI Use

Transparent and responsible AI use is crucial for maintaining trust with both customers and employees.

Strategies for building trust:
1. Use clear communication about AI use and its impact.
2. Provide options for customers to control their data and AI interactions.
3. Offer explanations for AI-driven decisions.
4. Establish channels for feedback and addressing concerns.
5. Demonstrate commitment to ethical AI use through actions and policies.

Implementation approaches:
1. Develop an AI transparency policy.

2. Create user-friendly interfaces for explaining AI decisions.
3. Provide regular updates to stakeholders about your AI practices.
4. Engage in open dialogue with customers and employees about AI use.
5. Participate in industry initiatives for responsible AI.

Challenges and Considerations in AI Ethics for Businesses

Implementing ethical AI practices can present unique challenges for businesses. Consider the following and their potential solutions.

Common challenges:
1. Balancing innovation with ethical constraints.
2. Keeping up with rapidly evolving AI technologies and ethical standards.
3. Addressing potential conflicts between business objectives and ethical considerations.
4. Ensuring consistent ethical practices across different departments and projects.
5. Limited resources for dedicated ethics teams, especially in smaller businesses.

Potential solutions:
1. Integrate ethics considerations into existing business processes.
2. Collaborate with other businesses or industry associations on AI ethics initiatives.
3. Leverage open-source ethics tools and frameworks.
4. Engage with external ethics experts or advisory boards.
5. Prioritize ethical considerations in AI vendor selection.

The Future of AI Ethics and Governance

As AI continues to evolve, so too will the ethical considerations and governance frameworks surrounding it. The rapid advancements in AI technology bring forth new opportunities and challenges, prompting ongoing discussions about its responsible development and deployment. Continuous dialogue and adaptation of governance frameworks are necessary to keep pace with AI's evolution and its impact on individuals, organizations, and society as a whole.

Emerging trends:
1. Increased regulatory focus on AI ethics and governance.
2. Development of industry-specific AI ethics standards.
3. Growing demand for AI auditing and certification.
4. The emergence of AI ethics as a competitive differentiator.
5. Integration of ethics considerations into AI development tools and platforms.

Preparing for the future:
1. Stay informed about evolving AI ethics standards and regulations.
2. Participate in industry discussions and initiatives on AI ethics.
3. Invest in ongoing training and education on AI ethics for your team.
4. Regularly review and update your AI ethics framework.
5. Consider appointing a chief AI ethics officer or similar role.

By prioritizing ethical considerations and implementing robust governance frameworks, businesses can harness the power of AI while maintaining trust, mitigating risks, and contributing to the responsible development of AI technologies. Remember, ethical AI is not just about compliance—it's also about building a sustainable and trustworthy foundation for your AI initiatives that align with your company's values and societal expectations.

In the final chapter, we'll look towards the future, exploring emerging AI technologies and their potential impact on businesses in the coming years.

Chapter 15

The Future of AI for Businesses

As we look towards the horizon of technological advancement, it's clear that AI will play an increasingly pivotal role in shaping the future of businesses. This chapter explores emerging AI technologies, potential challenges, and opportunities that lie ahead for businesses in the AI landscape.

Emerging AI Technologies Relevant to Businesses

Exploring emerging AI technologies offers new opportunities for innovation and efficiency in today's rapidly evolving technological landscape.

1. **Generative AI:**
    Application: Content creation, product design, and customer service.
    Potential Impact: Generative AI could revolutionize how businesses create marketing content, design products, and interact with customers. For example, a small marketing agency could use generative AI to quickly produce multiple versions of ad copy, significantly speeding up their creative process.

2. **Edge AI:**
    Application: Real-time data processing and decision-making at the point of data collection.
    Potential Impact: Edge AI could enable businesses to process data locally, reducing latency and improving privacy. For example, a retail store could use edge AI for real-time inventory management and personalized customer experiences without sending data to the cloud.

3. **Explainable AI (XAI):**
   Application: Providing clear explanations for AI-driven decisions.
   Potential Impact: XAI could increase trust in AI systems, particularly in industries like finance or healthcare, where decision transparency is crucial. A small lending company could use XAI to explain loan decisions to customers, improving satisfaction and regulatory compliance.

4. **Federated Learning:**
   Application: Collaborative AI model training without sharing raw data.
   Potential Impact: Federated learning could allow businesses to benefit from collective AI learning while maintaining data privacy. For example, small healthcare providers could collaborate on AI models for diagnosis without sharing sensitive patient data.

5. **AI-Powered Augmented and Virtual Reality:**
   Application: Enhanced customer experiences and employee training.
   Potential Impact: AR and VR powered by AI could transform how businesses interact with customers and train employees. A small furniture retailer could offer AI-powered AR apps, allowing customers to visualize products in their homes.

Preparing Your Business for Future AI Advancements

Preparing your business for future AI advancements involves the following proactive strategies.

1. **Cultivate a Data-Centric Culture:**

- Implement robust data collection and management practices.
- Encourage data-driven decision-making at all levels of the organization.

2. **Invest in Scalable AI Infrastructure:**
   - Choose cloud-based AI solutions that can grow with your business.
   - Ensure your IT infrastructure can support increasing AI workloads.

3. **Prioritize AI Education and Skills Development:**
   - Provide ongoing AI training for employees.
   - Consider partnering with educational institutions for AI talent development.

4. **Stay Informed About AI Trends and Regulations:**
   - Regularly review AI industry reports and attend relevant conferences.
   - Engage with industry associations focused on AI developments.

5. **Develop an AI Ethics Framework:**
   - Establish clear guidelines for ethical AI use in your organization.
   - Regularly review and update your ethics framework as AI technology evolves.

Potential Challenges and Opportunities

Examining the potential challenges and opportunities associated with AI implementation will provide insights into navigating its potentially transformative impact on your business operations and strategies.

Challenges:

1. Keeping pace with rapid AI advancements.
2. Managing the costs associated with AI implementation and maintenance.
3. Addressing potential job displacement and workforce transitions.
4. Ensuring data privacy and security in increasingly complex AI systems.
5. Navigating evolving AI regulations and compliance requirements.

Opportunities:
1. Leveling the playing field with larger competitors through AI-driven efficiencies.
2. Unlocking new revenue streams and business models enabled by AI.
3. Enhancing customer experiences through personalization and predictive services.
4. Improving decision-making with AI-powered analytics and insights.
5. Attracting top talent interested in working with cutting-edge AI technologies.

The Road Ahead: Key Takeaways for Businesses

The road ahead for businesses navigating AI integration involves the following strategies.

1. **Embrace Continuous Innovation:** The AI landscape will continue to evolve rapidly. Stay agile and open to new possibilities.

2. **Focus on Human-AI Collaboration:** The future of work will increasingly involve humans and AI working together. Prepare your workforce for this shift.

3. **Prioritize Ethical AI:** As AI becomes more pervasive, maintaining ethical standards will be crucial for building trust and avoiding reputational risks.

4. **Leverage AI for Sustainability:** Consider how AI can help your business contribute to sustainability goals and address environmental challenges.

5. **Collaborate and Share Knowledge:** Engage with other businesses, industry associations, and AI experts to share experiences and best practices.

As we stand on the brink of an AI-driven future, businesses have a unique opportunity to harness these technologies to drive growth, innovation, and competitive advantage. By staying informed, preparing strategically, and approaching AI adoption with a balance of enthusiasm and responsibility, businesses can position themselves to thrive in the AI-powered business landscape of tomorrow.

The future of AI for businesses is not just about adopting new technologies; it's about reimagining what's possible for your organization. As AI continues to evolve, it will open doors to new opportunities, efficiencies, and ways of working that we can scarcely imagine today. The businesses that embrace this future while navigating its challenges thoughtfully, will be well-positioned to lead in their industries and make a lasting impact in the years to come.

Chapter 16

Turnkey AI Solutions

In the modern business landscape, artificial intelligence (AI) is a powerful tool that can help small businesses streamline operations, enhance customer engagement, and drive growth. However, for many small business owners, the prospect of implementing AI can be overwhelming due to perceived complexity and cost. Turnkey AI solutions offer a practical entry point, providing pre-packaged, easy-to-deploy tools that cater to various business needs. This chapter explores how small businesses can leverage these solutions, with examples ranging from basic applications like content creation to advanced uses such as chatbots and marketing automation.

Understanding Turnkey AI Solutions

Turnkey AI solutions are designed to be user-friendly and require minimal customization, making them ideal for small businesses with limited technical resources. These solutions offer:

- **Ease of Use:** Intuitive interfaces and straightforward setup processes.
- **Cost-Effectiveness:** Reduced need for extensive development and infrastructure investment.
- **Quick Deployment:** Rapid implementation allows businesses to quickly benefit from AI capabilities.

Example: A small marketing agency might use a content generation tool like Jasper to automate the creation of blog posts and social media content, saving time and resources while maintaining quality.

Finding the Right Vendor

Selecting the right AI vendor is crucial for maximizing the benefits of turnkey solutions. Here's how small businesses can approach this process:

1. **Identify Business Needs:** Determine the specific challenges or opportunities you want to address with AI.

   Example: A boutique hotel might need an AI solution to manage guest inquiries and bookings more efficiently.

2. **Research Vendors:** Explore online resources to identify vendors offering solutions that align with your needs. Websites like FutureTools.io provide lists of AI tools categorized by function.

3. **Evaluate Solutions:** Assess the features, scalability, and integration capabilities of different solutions. Consider vendor reputation and customer feedback.

   Example: A small e-commerce business could evaluate AI-powered customer service platforms like Zendesk or Freshdesk to enhance support without increasing staff.

4. **Request Demos and Trials:** Engage vendors for demonstrations or trial periods to test the solution's effectiveness in your business environment.

5. **Consider Support and Training:** Ensure the vendor provides adequate support and training to facilitate smooth implementation and operation.

Conducting Your Own Research

In addition to vendor offerings, small business owners should conduct their own research to stay informed about AI trends and innovations:

- **Stay Updated:** Follow industry news, join AI forums, and participate in webinars to learn about the latest developments.

  Example: A small bakery could subscribe to newsletters focused on AI in retail to discover new tools for inventory management.

- **Network with Peers:** Connect with other small business owners who have implemented AI solutions to share experiences and insights.

- **Experiment with Free Tools:** Utilize free AI tools to gain hands-on experience and understand potential applications in your business.

  Example: A freelance writer might use Grammarly to enhance the quality and clarity of their content, benefiting from AI-driven grammar and style suggestions.

Implementing AI Solutions

Once a suitable AI solution is selected, careful planning and execution are essential for successful implementation:

1. **Set Clear Objectives:** Define what success looks like for your AI implementation. Establish measurable goals and key performance indicators (KPIs).

   Example: A local gym might aim to increase membership

retention by 15% using AI-driven personalized marketing campaigns.

2. **Prepare Your Team:** Ensure your team is on board with the AI initiative. Provide training and resources to help them understand and utilize the new technology effectively.

3. **Monitor and Evaluate:** Continuously monitor the performance of the AI solution against your objectives. Be prepared to make adjustments as needed to optimize outcomes.

   Example: A restaurant using AI for reservation management might track customer satisfaction and table turnover rates to assess effectiveness.

4. **Scale and Innovate:** As your business grows, explore opportunities to scale AI solutions or integrate additional AI technologies to further enhance operations.

   Example: A small retail chain that successfully implements AI for inventory management might expand its use to include AI-driven customer analytics for personalized shopping experiences.

Examples of Turnkey AI Applications

- **Basic Applications:**

  - **Content Creation:** Tools like Jasper and Copy.ai can automate writing tasks, from generating marketing copy to drafting emails, freeing up time for more strategic activities.

  - **Research:** AI tools like Answer Socrates and SparkToro help businesses understand customer interests and trends, enabling data-driven decision-making.

- **Advanced Applications:**

  - **Chatbots:** AI chatbots such as those offered by Sendbird provide 24/7 customer service, handling inquiries and sales tasks efficiently.

  - **Marketing Automation:** Platforms like HubSpot & Jasper automate marketing workflows, from email campaigns to customer segmentation, enhancing engagement and conversion rates.

  - **Predictive Analytics:** Solutions like SAP Predictive Analytics use machine learning to analyze customer data, enabling businesses to anticipate needs and tailor offerings.

Turnkey AI solutions empower small businesses to harness the benefits of AI without the complexities and costs of custom development. By selecting the right vendor, conducting thorough research, and strategically implementing AI solutions, small businesses can enhance their operations, improve customer experiences, and drive growth. With the right approach, AI becomes a valuable ally in navigating the competitive business landscape.

Conclusion

As we've explored throughout this book, Artificial Intelligence offers unprecedented opportunities for businesses of all sizes to innovate, compete, and thrive in an increasingly digital world. From automating routine tasks to enhancing customer experiences, from optimizing operations to driving strategic decision-making, AI has the potential to transform every aspect of your business.

As we've shown, the key to success in this AI-driven future lies not just in adopting the technology but in doing so strategically, ethically, and with a clear focus on your business objectives. Remember to start small, learn from your experiences, and gradually scale your AI initiatives.

As you move forward on your AI journey, maintain a balance between enthusiasm for AI's potential and a pragmatic, responsible approach to its implementation. Continually educate yourself and your team, stay abreast of AI developments, and don't hesitate to seek expertise when needed.

The AI revolution is here, and it's accessible to businesses of all sizes. With the knowledge and strategies provided in this book, you're now well-equipped to leverage AI as a powerful tool for achieving your business objectives, enhancing your value proposition, and better serving your customers.

The future is AI, and that future is now. Embrace it, shape it, and let it propel your business to new heights of success.

Glossary of AI Terms

1. **Artificial Intelligence (AI):** The simulation of human intelligence processes by machines, particularly computer systems.

2. **Automated Process:** A workflow or task executed by a machine or software without human intervention, often using AI technologies.

3. **Big Data:** Large and complex data sets that traditional data processing software cannot manage. AI tools analyze big data to uncover patterns and insights.

4. **Chatbot:** An AI program designed to simulate conversation with human users, especially over the Internet.

5. **Deep Learning:** A subset of machine learning that uses neural networks with many layers to analyze various factors of data.

6. **Large Language Model (LLM):** A type of AI algorithm trained on vast amounts of text data to understand and generate human-like text.

7. **Machine Learning (ML):** A branch of AI that focuses on the development of algorithms that allow computers to learn from and make predictions based

on data.

8. **Natural Language Processing (NLP):** A field of AI that enables computers to understand, interpret, and respond to human language.

9. **Predictive Analytics:** Techniques that use statistical algorithms and machine learning to identify the likelihood of future outcomes based on historical data.

10. **Robotic Process Automation (RPA):** The use of software robots or "bots" to automate repetitive, rule-based tasks traditionally performed by humans.

11. **Supervised Learning:** A type of machine learning where the model is trained on a labeled dataset.

12. **Unsupervised Learning:** A type of machine learning that uses input data without labeled responses to find patterns and relationships.

www.ingramcontent.com/pod-product-compliance
Lightning Source LLC
LaVergne TN
LVHW051713050326
832903LV00032B/4177